I0236268

Healthy
BENJI

International Eats

Dr. Benji's real name is Dr. Verna R. Benjamin-Lambert

International Eats

© 2012 by Dr. Verna R. Benjamin-Lambert

All rights reserved. No part of this publication may be reproduced or transmitted in any form or by any means, electronic or mechanical, including photocopying, recording, or by any information storage and retrieval system, without the prior written permission from the publisher or the authors, except by reviewers who may quote brief excerpts in connection with a review in a newspaper, magazine or electronic publication. Contact the publisher for information on foreign rights.

Library of Congress Control Number: 1817813

ISBN: 978-0-9910361-9-6

Printed in the United States of America

INTERNATIONAL EATS
POTLUCK AT THE SCHOOL

BY
DR. BENJI
ILLUSTRATED BY ARASHI YANG

HEALTHY READING FOR HEALTHY EATING!
BOOK FOR EARLY READERS

Health Intelligence, LLC.

To Parents and Teachers

The Healthy Benji book series brings excitement through reading about a variety of nutritious foods. Children will learn the value of various fruits and vegetables and understand how to make strategic choices as they nourish their bodies. The stories are designed to expose children to a wide array of food choices and for them to enjoy being a part of the preparation process.

Questions are asked at the end of each story to ensure that children understand and gain knowledge from what is read. Teachers and parents are encouraged to assist children in preparing meals using fresh fruits and vegetables to make dishes that children will find enjoyable to prepare and delicious to eat. When children become a part of the preparation process they will be more likely to try new things.

Throughout the Healthy Benji books series meaningful family connections are emphasized along with friendship, responsibility, manners, helpfulness, hygiene, appreciation and respect for others.

The Healthy Benji Book Series will help children develop healthy eating habits at a very early age. Through reading about and practicing healthy habits our children will have the best foundation possible to enjoy a wholesome and happy life.

LET'S START HERE! IT'S COOL TO BE HEALTHY

TABLE OF CONTENTS

Healthy Recipes and More (cont.)

CHAPTER 1

WHAT'S A POTLUCK?

After school one day, the principal said, "We are going to have a potluck dinner. This year's theme is International Food, so we'd like each family to bring something from their culture. There are flyers by the back door to tell you the time and place. Please take one on your way out and we look forward to seeing everyone at the potluck dinner."

On the way out, Healthy Benji turned to Nadia and said, "What's a potluck?"

"A potluck is a party where everyone brings something different to eat. Then, everyone gets to try whatever food they want to taste," described Nadia.

Healthy Benji's mom added, "Everyone is going to bring something that is part of their culture. Then we can sample different kinds of food. You never know what you like until you try it. And, you could learn more about other cultures and other people. Trying food from another place is just one easy way of learning about other people. It's fun to see how other people cook, eat, and what kinds of foods they choose."

Healthy Benji liked the idea of a potluck.

Healthy Benji's dad said, "Not just that, but you would also learn a little more about your own culture. You might have to do a little research to find the recipe for whatever you are going to cook. Plus, you might have to find specific ingredients at a special ethnic market." Healthy Benji thought that could be kind of cool.

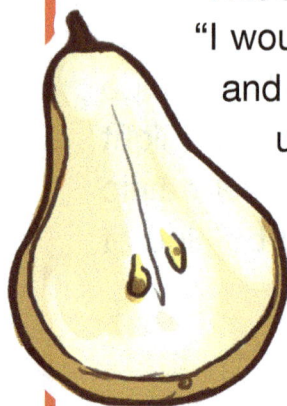

"This sounds like a great idea," said Healthy Benji. "I would love to know more about other people and the different cultures. I think I usually end up eating the same kind of food all the time, only from my culture. It will be good to try something different. Actually, it will be great to try lots of different things."

The whole family agreed to work together to prepare for the potluck dinner.

The flyer for the International Food potluck stated that all families should R.S.V.P to Mrs. Styler so she could keep track of how many people were coming. She wanted to make sure she had enough tables and chairs set up in the gymnasium.

When Healthy Benji's mom called Mrs. Styler, she said that almost fifty people had already responded that they were coming. This was going to be a big event! Healthy Benji and Nadia couldn't wait.

CHAPTER 2
DECISIONS, DECISIONS...

Healthy Benji wondered what he and Nadia could make for the potluck.

"Well, maybe we should look up some recipes on the internet," said Nadia. "We are African American, so we'd probably make something called soul food."

Healthy Benji had an idea, too. "Or, we can ask Mom and Dad what kinds of foods they ate when they were young kids. I'm sure grandma and papa made interesting meals at their house. Maybe they have some ideas too."

Healthy Benji and Nadia knew just where to start their research.

Healthy Benji and Nadia talked with their parents, their grandparents, and they even did some soul food research on the internet. After sharing their information, they had a few things to cook.

Over the next few weeks, the family planned out their recipes, took a trip to the market and the ethnic food store, and worked together to get their dishes ready for the International Potluck dinner.

Healthy Benji and Nadia worked in the kitchen with Mom and Dad to make their soul food dishes for the potluck. They cut vegetables, breaded the chicken, cooked the beans, and baked the dessert. Healthy Benji didn't even have to be reminded of the kitchen safety rules. He washed his hands before cooking, he was very safe with all the kitchen tools, and he made sure he helped to clean up when they were finished. The dishes turned out fantastic.

They all took a taste to make sure things tasted just right. The family was ready for the potluck. They packed up their dishes and headed off to the potluck.

CHAPTER 3
FOOD FESTIVITIES!

The potluck dinner was held in the gymnasium at school. When Healthy Benji and Nadia entered, they saw decorations. The tables were set up with fancy tablecloths and decorations. There were streamers and balloons of all different colors, and lots of chairs. There were plenty of tables for each family to display their food. People were arriving and chatting, kids were running around, and music was playing in the background. Some people were even dancing!

Soon everyone arrived. All the dishes were set out and ready to be served. The gymnasium smelled yummy with all the different kinds of food, so everyone was growing hungrier by the minute. The principal thanked everyone for coming.

The crowd took their seats at the tables, grew quiet, and followed the principal in a pre-celebration moment of reflection. After the moment of reflection everyone talked and got to know each other.

When the meet and greet session was over, the guests lined up near the tables to sample the variety of food. Most people had labeled their food, so you knew exactly what you were eating. That was a good thing, because some of the foods might look like one thing, but might actually be something else!

CHAPTER 4
ASIAN FLAVORS

Healthy Benji was happy to try everything at the potluck dinner. He took a plate, silverware, and a napkin and started wandering by each table. First, he came to the table that had **Chinese** food. There were homemade egg rolls, a vegetable and beef stir fry, white rice and fried rice, lots of sautéed vegetables, chicken chow mein, a pot of wonton soup, low mein noodles, and sweet and sour chicken. Oh, yeah, and fortune cookies. Everything looked yummy. Healthy Benji took a sample of several items. He wanted to make sure he didn't take too much food because he did not want to waste anything.

The next table had a large sign that read: "Japanese food". It looked a lot like Chinese food to Healthy Benji. There were different kinds of sushi, which was a tiny bite sized chunk of fresh fish, rice, and vegetables wrapped in a seaweed wrapper. There were soy beans.

Healthy Benji knew he liked those, so he put a few on his plate. There was also miso soup, grilled fish, yakitori or chicken skewers, and fried ice cream. Healthy Benji was eager to try all these new foods. He had never actually had much Japanese food, except the soy beans. He was pretty sure he'd like the fried ice cream.

Healthy Benji went to the next table too, because he had never even heard of **Thai** food before. This food was from Thailand, and Healthy Benji had never been there. It looked a lot like some of the other dishes he had seen, but he knew that it probably tasted a little different.

He saw a dish that had noodles, shrimp, chicken, onions, peppers, scrambled eggs, tofu, bean sprouts, peanuts, and a lime slice on top. Healthy Benji read the label "Pad Thai."

"Hmmm, a healthy mixture of food on one plate," he thought.

There was another dish that had a label that read: Khao Phat Kai. Below the name of the dish, someone had written what it was – fried rice with chicken.

"I was just about to ask what Khao Phat Kai meant," Healthy Benji said to Nadia.

"Me too," said Nadia. "I had no idea what that could be."

Then Healthy Benji saw something called "Wing Bean Salad."

"I thought I knew what bean salad was, but I'm not so sure about Wing Bean Salad. Do those beans have wings?" questioned Healthy Benji.

The lady behind the table said, "No, No, those beans don't have wings. They are called wing beans because they are blanched and tossed with coconut milk, roasted chili paste, toasted coconut, tamarind, palm sugar, and peanuts."

"Sounds good," he said, as the woman put a sample on his plate. He and Nadia sat at the table and ate before moving on to the next table.

CHAPTER 5
HEALTHY BENJI'S ITALIAN FAVORITES

Healthy Benji was happy because the next table was the **Italian** table. This was one of Healthy Benji's favorite kinds of food. He loved pizza, and he loved noodles.

Nadia knew about Healthy Benji's love of Italian food, and she said, "Now, Healthy Benji, go easy on the Italian. Save room for some other countries, too!" Of course, there was pizza and several different kinds too. He saw some of his favorites, like pepperoni, sausage, and cheese. But, he also saw some that he had never tried before.

There were so many choices - pineapple and ham, onion and sun dried tomato, or bacon and olive. There was pizza with thin crust, pizza with thick crust, pizza with red sauce, pizza with white sauce, and even pizza with garlic sauce. It was so hard to choose which kind to try! Healthy Benji took a slice of spinach and goat cheese pizza with mushrooms. It looked really yummy.

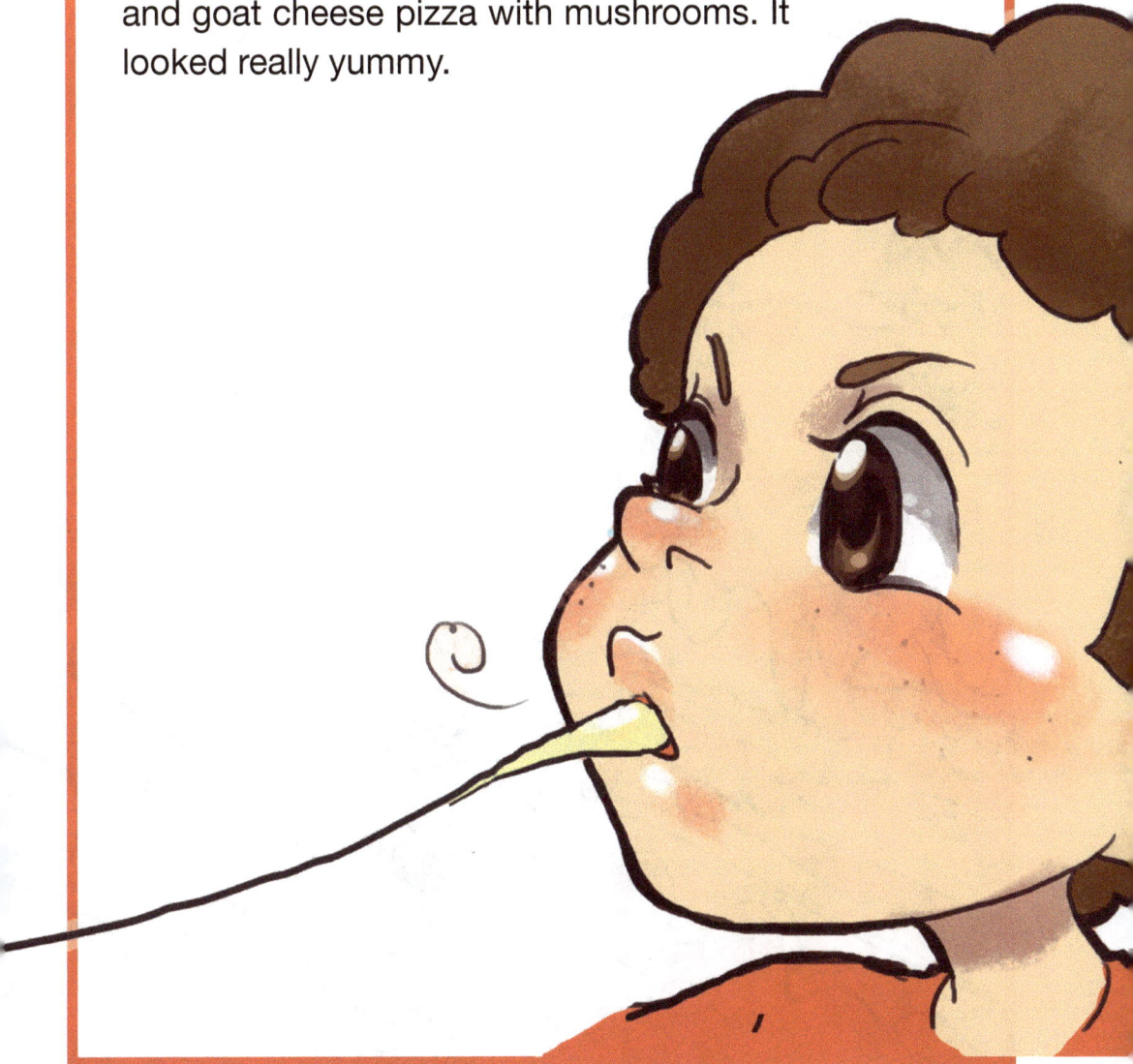

There was also a variety of pastas and sauces. There was penne with red sauce, linguini with Alfredo sauce, and spaghetti with meatballs. Somebody made lasagna, which had layers of pasta, sauce, and cheese. Some of the lasagna had vegetables in it, and some had meat in it. So many choices!

Healthy Benji knew it would be hard not to eat all the good food, so he took just a little of the Italian food. Plus, he didn't want to look greedy.

Another Italian family made chicken with parmesan cheese and vegetable soup with little pieces of pasta in it. The lady serving said the pasta was called ditalini. Healthy Benji thought that was a silly name.

Healthy Benji had a hard time choosing what to taste. He wanted a little bit of everything, but he knew he could never eat all that.

CHAPTER 6
OTHER EUROPEAN DELIGHTS

Healthy Benji was happy to greet Albert at the next table. "Hi there, Albert," said Healthy Benji.

"Hey there, Healthy Benji," he answered.

"What nationality are you?"

"I'm half **Irish** and half German," said Albert. "But I'm serving Irish food today."

"Okay," said Healthy Benji. "What do you have for me to try?"

Healthy Benji talked about the food they were serving. "First, there's Irish soda bread with raisins in it. You can add a little butter if you want, but it doesn't need anything on it. Then, we've got roasted potatoes, cabbage, and corned beef."

Healthy Benji had never had Irish soda bread or corned beef before, so he tried a taste of each. He was starting to feel full. He had been sampling a lot of food.

Next, there was a small table that had a few **Polish** dishes on it. Healthy Benji's friend from school, Becky, was Polish, and her family had made the dishes at this table. Healthy Benji knew what pierogies were – little noodle pockets filled with cheese or potatoes, or both. "What are these pierogies filled with?" Healthy Benji asked Becky's mom.

She answered by pointing at the different bowls. "These are filled with cheese and bacon. Those are filled with potatoes and onions. I hope you like them." She told Healthy Benji to try them with some cooked cabbage or sour cream. He liked them. Nadia liked them, too.

But, that wasn't all that Becky's mom was serving. She also had polish sausage, which she called kielbasa, and some Polish desserts. One of the desserts was called paczek. It was a donut filled with fruit jelly. And, there was something called sernik – it was an unusual kind of Polish cheesecake. Healthy Benji just loved donuts and cheesecake. He was happy to try the Polish desserts. Nadia tried them, too.

The **German** table was next. Healthy Benji's friend John was there with his family, serving up some German favorites. "Hey!" said Healthy Benji.

"Hey!" Said John. They goofed around for a few minutes, and then John asked Healthy Benji if he would like to try some German food.

"Sure," said Healthy Benji. "What should I try?"

John showed Healthy Benji all of the choices and described each one.

There was German sausage, also called bratwurst, which looked sort of like the Polish sausage at the last table. There was sauerkraut made from cabbage, and there was a German hot potato salad that was made with potatoes, bacon, celery, and onions. For dessert, there was apple strudel. Mmmm. Healthy Benji liked German food.

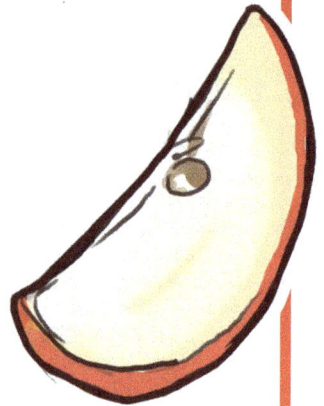

CHAPTER 7
MIDDLE EASTERN MUNCHIES

Right next to the German food table was the **Mediterranean** food table. This food was Greek, and Healthy Benji knew a few of items on the table. There were gyros – pita bread with shaved lamb slices, onion, tomato, and a white sauce on top.

"What kind of sauce is that?" Healthy Benji asked the man behind the table.

"It's called tzatziki sauce," he said. "It's made of plain yogurt with cucumber. Would you like to taste it?" The man gave him a taste of the sauce on a small spoon. Healthy Benji liked it.

"Thanks," said Healthy Benji.

"You're welcome," said the man.

The man also showed Healthy Benji and Nadia that he had a Greek salad with olives and feta cheese, samples of lamb chops, a Moroccan vegetable soup, and chicken vegetable kabobs. Kabobs are vegetables and meat on wooden sticks. Everything looked delicious, but Healthy Benji and Nadia were both getting too full to eat anything else.

"Thank you for the sample," said Healthy Benji.

Middle Eastern food was the theme of the next table. The woman serving the food explained that hummus was a tasty dip made with chick peas. You could dip pita bread or vegetables in it. She also had falafel made with chick peas.

"That looks like a pancake," said Healthy Benji.

"It is a bit like a pancake. A vegetable pancake," said the woman.

The woman showed Nadia a bowl of tabouleh made with bulgur, tomato, and parsley, a plate of chicken with lemon and garlic, and a dish made with some lentil beans. For dessert, there was buklawa, which is a pastry made with layers and layers of crust and nuts. Everything looked quite yummy. Healthy Benji wished he wasn't so full.

"Thanks for telling us all about your food. It was very nice to meet you," Healthy Benji told the woman.

"You're welcome. It was lovely talking to you too," she said.

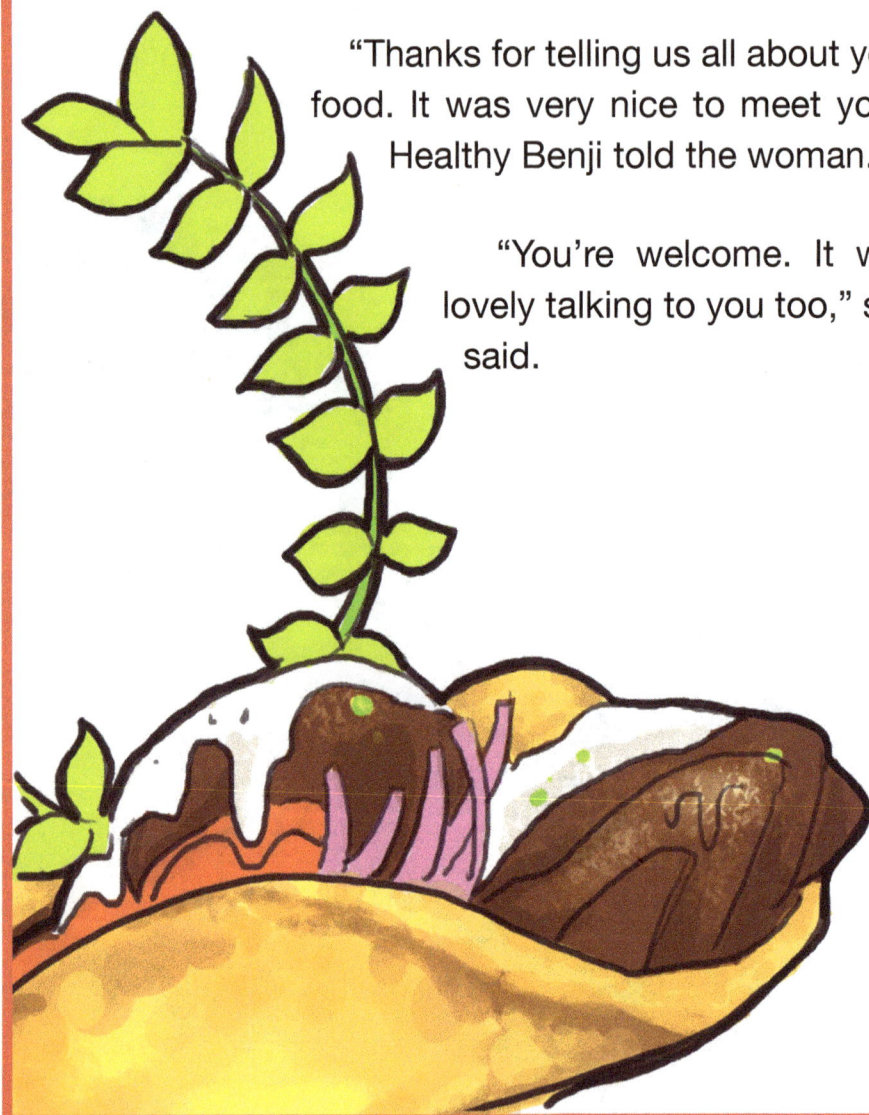

"I'm not sure I'm going to be able to taste everything at this potluck," Healthy Benji told Nadia.

"Me neither," said Nadia. "There's just too much good stuff to try!"

Healthy Benji had a brilliant idea. "Maybe we can make a plate of some samples to take home with us."

"Good thinking," said Nadia.

"Or maybe we could ask people for the recipes, and we could make some of the food at home," said Healthy Benji.

"Good thinking again," said Nadia.

"Or, we could go to a restaurant that serves that kind of food," said Healthy Benji.

Nadia jumped in and said, "Healthy Benji, you've got all the ideas." They both giggled.

"We still have four tables of food left to go," said Nadia.

"Yes," said Healthy Benji. "And we don't want to waste any food. It would be rude to throw food away."

Nadia agreed. "Absolutely, it would be rude. In some cultures, it's important that you eat whatever is served or what you put on your plate. We wouldn't want anyone to feel mad or sad if we didn't eat their food."

"Right," said Healthy Benji. "Well, maybe we could just go around and talk to people and meet them, and find out what they are serving. We don't have to eat. After all, it's not a good idea to stuff yourself. But, we could still learn about their culture."

"That's the best idea you've had," Nadia told Healthy Benji.

CHAPTER 8
ALOHA AND FIESTA

Off they went, to meet people and learn about the rest of the cultures at the potluck. The **Hawaiian** table was next. It had a dish of pineapple, rice, and pork. There was real tuna, not like the kind from the can, and there was a plate of shrimp.

Healthy Benji didn't know anyone who was Hawaiian, and he didn't recognize the people serving the food. Healthy Benji overheard some people at that table talking about how people who live in Hawaii eat a lot of seafood because it is plentiful and healthy.

There was also a tray of Hawaiian fruits like mango, papaya, and guava. The man at the table said that since the weather is so warm and humid in Hawaii, fruit grows very well and is very common. Healthy Benji knew he liked fruit, and he wanted to taste the fresh flavor of these Hawaiian trays.

The man gave Healthy Benji some samples and he tried a small bite. He did like the Hawaiian fruit. He'd have to make sure to ask his mom to get some at the grocery store next time.

There was a **Mexican** table full of food too. Healthy Benji's friend Hayden was Mexican, and Healthy Benji had been to their house to eat before. The food they served was always so yummy. Hayden's mom and dad had made homemade salsa, cooked chicken with rice and beans, mini burritos, tacos, and fajitas with beef strips and vegetables.

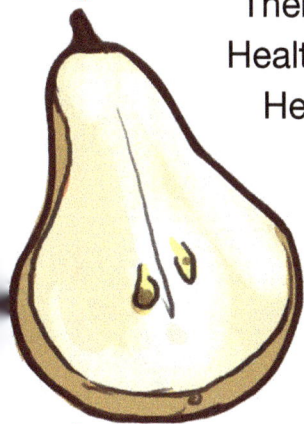

Healthy Benji saw something he had never seen before, and asked his friend Hayden what it was.

"Those are empanadas," said Hayden. "They're like pastry that's stuffed with ground beef and cheese. They're downright yummy."

Healthy Benji thought that sounded quite good. He said, "It's kind of like a cheeseburger pie!"

"Right," said Hayden. The boys giggled.

"And, what is that?" Healthy Benji said, pointing to a platter.

"Those are tamales," said Hayden. "Each one has corn dough and vegetables cooked inside a leaf wrapper. Sometimes they have meat in them, or jalapenos or chilies, or fruit or whatever, but these have vegetables like green peppers and onions."

Healthy Benji told Hayden he was too full to eat much more. "Well, you'll just have to come over to my house for dinner some night, and we'll make tamales," said Hayden.

"Great," said Healthy Benji.

CHAPTER 9
A TASTE OF THE SOUTH

Healthy Benji's parents were at their **Soul Food** table. Healthy Benji and Nadia stopped by to say hello. "How do people like the food we made?" Healthy Benji asked.

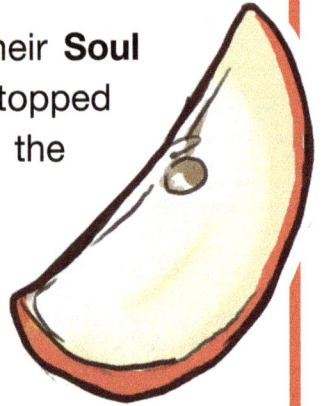

"Great!" Said Healthy Benji's mom. "Everything is going quickly."

They made ham hocks, fried okra, black eyed peas, fried chicken, cornbread, greens, and rice.

"How's the rest of the International Potluck?" wondered Mom.

"Oh my goodness, there's so much food to try, and everything is so good!" said Nadia. "I keep seeing friends from school. It's so much fun."

"Good," said Mom. "I'm glad you are having fun."

"We've got a few more tables to visit," said Nadia.

"Right, let's go. See you later, Mom and Dad," said Healthy Benji.

"I hope you are using your manners," said Mom.

"We are," said Nadia and Healthy Benji at the same time. And, off they went to the next table.

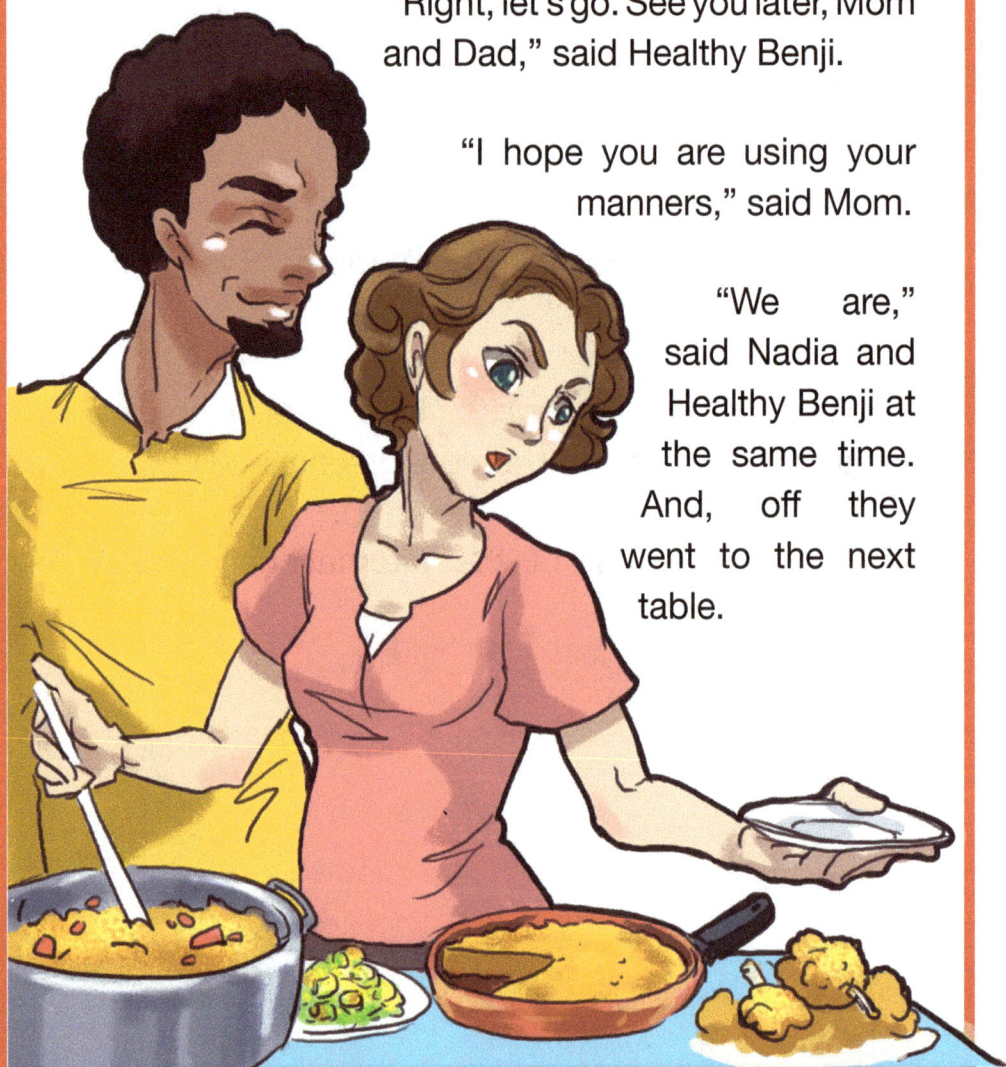

Healthy Benji and Nadia's last stop was the **Cajun** food table that was right next to the soul food table. They learned this kind of food was common in Louisiana. Healthy Benji knew the people serving the food since they were his neighbors, Mr. And Mrs. Bonet! He said 'hello' and asked what kind of food they had to share.

Mr. Bonet said that there was a delicacy called crawfish, which looked like mini lobsters! He also showed Healthy Benji and Nadia the red beans and sausage, and two kinds of soup – one was called Jambalaya (which had shrimp, onions, tomatoes, celery, and spices) and the other one was called Seafood Gumbo. Healthy Benji thought the words Jambalaya and Gumbo were kind of funny.

Mrs. Bonet showed Healthy Benji and Nadia their special desserts too. There was old fashioned lemonade, a delicious looking pecan pie, and a 7 Up pound cake. Healthy Benji had never heard of a cake made with pop before! He had to try it. Also, there were two New Orleans specialties called pralines, which are a special candy made with nuts, and beignets, which are like donuts.

Finally, Mr. Bonet introduced a dessert called a king cake. He told Healthy Benji and Nadia that the king cake was special because it is made and served during Mardi Gras or carnival season. Sometimes there is a special toy or trinket baked inside the cake. Whoever gets the trinket will have special privileges and obligations. Healthy Benji liked the idea of a special tradition like that. He liked all the samples at the Cajun food table. Nadia did too.

CHAPTER 10
PERFECT END TO A PERFECT DAY

Healthy Benji and Nadia had seen all the tables and sampled a lot of food. They had learned many new things about lots of cultures. Healthy Benji and Nadia sat down to rest and let their food settle while they chatted with some friends.

"What was your favorite?" Healthy Benji asked his friend.

"Hmmm," he said. "It's so hard to choose. Everything was so yummy. I liked the pizza, of course. But I also liked the beignets – they are just like donuts!"

Healthy Benji agreed that all the food was delicious and said, "I still like pizza too, but those Mexican empanadas were pretty tasty, too. I also liked the 7 Up cake – that was awesome." Nadia said that she liked the different kinds of Chinese noodles. Hayden liked the gyros.

"It's cool," said Healthy Benji. "Everybody likes something different!"

After resting, they played a game of kickball. Hayden and Healthy Benji helped organize the teams. The game was fun! Everyone played together nicely, the teams took turns kicking and fielding, and followed the rules. Healthy Benji almost had a homerun. Healthy Benji's team won, but it didn't matter because they were having so much fun. At the end of the game, the teams lined up and shook hands.

The kids headed back inside to help clean up the International Potluck. Everyone pitched in to help. Healthy Benji and Nadia cleaned off the tables and threw away trash. Healthy Benji and Hayden collected the recyclable bottles and cans and plastic. The parents packed up the left-over food, and others helped take down the decorations.

In no time, everything was all cleaned up, and the hall was looking spotless. The principal got on the microphone, "I want to thank you all for coming to our first annual International Potluck. The food was delicious, and the chats were great. I thank everyone who brought food to share, and I thank you all for the help setting up and cleaning up. I think this has been a huge success. I hope to do it again next year. Thanks, and have a splendid rest
of the day!"

On the way home, Healthy Benji and Nadia couldn't stop talking about the potluck. "What a great idea," said Healthy Benji. "I mean, to get everyone together like that and to get to know people in a different way. I learned a lot about different cultures and tried some new things that I *really* like."

Nadia agreed. "I know. It's like, when you know more about something or someone; you have a greater respect for the person and their culture. Sometimes when you don't know people, you don't know the nifty things you are missing."

"It's funny," said Healthy Benji. "I didn't even really know what culture some of my friends came from until today."

Healthy Benji's mom agreed but added, "I'm glad you enjoyed it and learned something about other cultures. But, there's more to a culture than just tasting their food. It's really more about getting to know people, their beliefs and what's most important to them. Food is only one way of bringing people together."

"Well then, we have a lot more to learn!" shouted Healthy Benji.

"That's Right!" said Nadia.

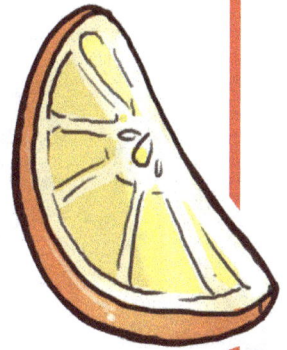

Healthy Benji said, "All I know is, I have eaten enough food to last me for the whole week. I feel like I have noodles, and vegetables, and cheese, and desserts coming out of my ears. Maybe you should call me 'Cheesy Stuffed Healthy Benji'." The whole family laughed.

They enjoyed the rest of their day together without even eating a thing. They were all too full of International goodies from the potluck dinner.

DISCUSSION QUESTIONS:

What is your ethnicity? If you don't know, ask your parents.

In your culture, what are some of the authentic or traditional dishes?

What kind of ethnic food would you like to try? Find a restaurant that serves that food or find some recipes and make some ethnic food at home.

What foods from the story are your favorites?

Pick a culture from the story. Do a little research to learn something new about that culture!

What does respect mean? How can you show respect to someone of another culture? How can you show respect for your own culture?

What kind of food traditions do you have with your family? Think about holidays, birthdays, or family meal favorites.

HEALTHY RECIPES AND MORE

SWEET POTATO PANCAKES

Ingredients:
- 1 ½ cups of all-purpose flour
- 3 ½ teaspoons of baking powder
- 1 teaspoon of salt
- ½ teaspoon of ground nutmeg
- ½ teaspoon of cinnamon
- 1 ¼ cups of cooked sweet potatoes – mashed
- 2 eggs – beaten
- 1 ½ cups of milk
- ¼ cup of butter – melted

Preparation:
1. In a large bowl mix flour, baking powder, salt, nutmeg, and cinnamon.
2. In another bowl combine sweet potatoes, eggs, milk, and butter.
3. Combine wet and dry ingredients, and stir until batter is moist.
4. Grease skillet with cooking spray, and turn on to medium heat.
5. Drop batter by tablespoons and fry on the skillet.
6. Flip once so pancake is browned on both sides.
7. Remove from skillet and serve with maple syrup or cinnamon sugar.

Makes about 24 pancakes.

DID YOU KNOW...?

- Sweet potatoes have lots of fiber, especially with the skin on.

- Sweet potatoes have nutrients like potassium, iron, and vitamin B-6.

- Sweet potatoes are the official vegetable for North Carolina.

- Sweet potatoes can be:
  - ◈ Baked
  - ◈ Steamed
  - ◈ Boiled
  - ◈ Micro-waved
  - ◈ Fried
  - ◈ Juiced
  - ◈ Pureed
  - ◈ Eaten raw

- George Washington grew sweet potatoes on his farm in Virginia.

PIGGY BUNS

Ingredients:
- 1 apple – diced
- 2 eggs – beaten
- 1 cup of milk
- ½ tablespoon of cinnamon
- 8 whole wheat hot dog buns
- 1 cup of cornflakes – crushed
- 8 turkey sausage links

Preparation:
1. Prepare sausage according to package directions and set aside.
2. Crush cornflakes on a plate and set aside.
3. Crack egg in bowl, add milk, and cinnamon. Beat well.
4. Grease skillet with cooking spray, and turn burner on to medium heat.
5. Open each hot dog bun. Dip in egg mixture to cover both sides. Then dip in cornflake crumbs to coat.
6. Place on skillet. Flip once until lightly brown on both sides.
7. Remove from skillet and place on plate to cool. Place sausage in the bun, add diced apples, and maple syrup. Enjoy like a hot dog!

Makes 8 Piggy Buns.

DID YOU KNOW...?

- Don't peel your apple! Most of the fiber and many antioxidants are found in the apple peel.

- The largest apple picked weighed three pounds.

- Red Delicious, Golden Delicious, Granny Smith, Gala and Fuji are the top five apples eaten in the United States.

- Apples are a member of the rose family, along with pears, peaches, plums and cherries.

- One apple has five grams of fiber.

- Apples are fat, sodium, and cholesterol free.

ANTIOXIDANT MUFFINS

Ingredients:

- 1 ½ cups of all-purpose flour
- ¾ cup of white sugar
- ½ teaspoon of salt
- 2 teaspoons of baking powder
- 1/3 cup of vegetable oil
- 1 egg – beaten
- 1/3 cup of milk
- 1 cup of blueberries
- ½ cup of raspberries
- ½ cup of blackberries

Preparation:

1. Preheat oven to 400 degrees.
2. Line muffin tin with muffin cups.
3. Combine flour, sugar, salt, and baking powder.
4. Place oil into a 1 cup measuring cup. Add the beaten egg and enough milk to fill the cup. Add to flour mixture.
5. Fold in blueberries, raspberries, and blackberries.
6. Fill muffin cups to the top with mix.
7. Bake for 20 to 25 minutes.

Makes about 12 muffins.

DID YOU KNOW...?

- America's favorite muffin is blueberry.

- July is national blueberry month.

- The blueberry is the official state fruit of New Jersey.

- There are over 200 species of raspberries.

- Raspberries can be red, black, yellow, or purple.

- Blackberries are high in Vitamin C and fiber.

- Blackberries are helpful in the treatment of stomach problems.

NO-YOLK, MICRO-SCRAMBLED EGGS

Ingredients:
- 3 eggs – separated (use only the whites)
- ¼ cup of milk
- ¼ cup of green pepper – diced
- ¼ cup of tomatoes – diced
- ¼ cup of mushrooms – chopped
- ¼ cup of shredded cheddar cheese

Preparation:
1. In a microwaveable bowl, place two egg whites, add milk, and blend with a fork.
2. Add cheese and vegetables to the egg mix.
3. Microwave for 2-3 minutes.
4. Allow eggs to cool for about 1 minute.

Makes 1- 2 servings.

DID YOU KNOW...?

- There are at least 25,000 varieties of tomatoes.
- Tomatoes have been called "wolf peach," "a plump thing with a navel," and "the apple of love."
- Mushrooms do not need sunshine to grow and thrive.
- The pepper is actually a fruit, not a vegetable.
- Peppers come in many colors, including green, yellow, orange, red, brown, and purple.

SUPER SWEET FRUIT SALAD

Ingredients:

- 1 cup strawberries – diced
- 1 cup blueberries
- 1 cup red grapes – diced
- 1 nectarine – diced
- 1 pear – diced
- 1 apple – diced
- ½ cup of honey
- 1 ½ cups of fruit juice (grape, apple, orange, cranberry, or any other kind – you choose!)
- ½ lemon or ½ an orange
- *Optional:* nuts, raisins, or other dried fruit

Preparation:

1. Wash fruit. Chop or dice each fruit into bite-sized pieces and place in a large bowl.
2. Pour juice on top and add honey.
3. Squeeze the juice of ½ of one lemon or ½ of one orange on top of the fruit.
4. Stir gently until fruit and juices are mixed well.

Makes about 8-10 servings.

DID YOU KNOW...?

- Nectarines don't have fuzz but peaches do.

- Nectarines are an excellent source of vitamins A and C.

- In China, it's bad luck to share a pear.

- Pear's nickname is "butter fruit."

- Grapes can come in many colors, like white, red, black, blue, green, purple and golden.

- Grapes are on the top ten list of favorite fruits.

- Over 80% of strawberries are grown in California.

- Strawberries are hand-picked because they are so fragile.

COWBOY BANANA SMOOTHIES

Ingredients:
- 2 bananas
- 6-8 strawberries
- 1 cup of peach yogurt
- 1 ½ cups of mango juice or mango nectar

Preparation:
1. Fill blender pitcher 1/3 of the way with ice cubes.
2. Pour mango juice over ice.
3. Add yogurt, bananas, and strawberries.
4. Cover and blend until liquefied.

Makes about 6 servings.

DID YOU KNOW...?

- Bananas, apples, and watermelons float in water.
- The average American eats 27 pounds of bananas each year!
- An individual banana is called a finger. A bunch of bananas is called a hand.
- Bananas are a good source of vitamin B6, which your brain needs to function properly and make you wise.
- Mangoes are related to cashews and pistachios
- The mango is a symbol of love in India.

MELON KABOBS AND YOGURT DIP

Ingredients:
- ½ of a honeydew melon
- ½ of a small watermelon
- ½ of a cantaloupe
- ½ of a mush melon
- 1 ½ cups vanilla yogurt
- ½ cup honey
- Juice of ½ lime

Preparation:
1. Slice off rind of each melon and cut into large bite-sized chunks.
2. Place melon in various patterns on wooden skewers.
3. In a small bowl, mix yogurt, honey, and lime.
4. Use skewers to dip melon chunks in yogurt dip.
5. Try other fruits too!

Makes 6-8 servings.

DID YOU KNOW...?

- Honeydew melons are also known as temptation melons.

- Honeydews are the sweetest of all melons when ripe.

- Cantaloupe is a great source of Vitamin A.

- Most cantaloupes are grown in Arizona or California.

- Watermelon is 92% water.

- Watermelon is usually red, but there is also a yellow variety.

SWEET & CRUNCHY VEGGIE SALAD

Ingredients:
- 4 cups of lettuce – shredded
- 1 cup of raw green beans – diced
- 1 cup of raw carrots – diced
- ½ cup of raw jicama – diced
- ½ cup of raw white onion – diced
- ½ cup of blue cheese chunks
- ½ cup of dried cranberries
- ¼ cup of pecans – chopped

  Dressing:
- ¼ cup of maple syrup
- ½ cup of white vinegar
- 1 tablespoon of sugar
- Juice of ½ lemon

Preparation:
1. Slice the vegetables, place them in a large bowl, and set aside.
2. In a separate bowl, make dressing: Mix vinegar, maple syrup, sugar, and lemon. Blend well.
3. Add cheese, dried fruit, and nuts.
4. Pour dressing over salad mix and toss until well coated.

Makes about 4-6 servings.

DID YOU KNOW...?

- Lettuce is a member of the sunflower family.

- Dark green lettuce leaves are more nutritious than lighter green leaves.

- Green beans are a great source of fiber.

- The heaviest carrot on record was nearly 19 pounds.

- The longest carrot on record was 16 feet 10.5 inches long.

- Jicama is a member of the potato family and can weigh up to 50 pounds.

- Onions can heal blisters.

FUN FIESTA SALSA

Ingredients:
- 4 medium sized tomatoes – diced
- ½ green pepper – diced
- ½ red pepper – diced
- ½ yellow pepper – diced
- 1 white onion – diced
- ½ cup of vinegar
- 1 tablespoon of cilantro
- 1 teaspoon of garlic salt
- 1 teaspoon of black pepper
- Juice of ½ lemon or ½ lime
- Tortilla chips – like blue corn chips, or quinoa chips

Preparation:
1. Dice vegetables and place in a large bowl.
2. Pour vinegar over vegetables.
3. Add cilantro, garlic salt, black pepper, and lemon or lime juice.
4. Mix well, chill, and serve with tortilla chips.

Makes about 10-12 servings.

DID YOU KNOW...?

- Peppers are actually fruits that form on the plant after it flowers.

- Peppers can be green, red, yellow, and orange.

- Sometimes peppers can even be white, purple, blue, and brown, depending on when they are harvested.

- Tomatoes are actually a fruit.

- Tomato season is from June to November.

- Onion can help remove warts.

- Onions can soothe an insect bite.

HAYDEN'S TASTY GUAC

Ingredients:

- 2 avocados – sliced
- 2 tomatoes – diced
- 1 yellow onion – diced
- 1 can sweet corn – drained
- 1 can black beans – drained
- Juice of ½ lemon
- Garlic salt
- Black pepper
- ¼ cup white vinegar

Preparation:

1. In a large bowl, mash avocados with a fork.
2. Add tomatoes, onions, sweet corn, and beans.
3. Add juice of ½ lemon, garlic salt, black pepper, and vinegar.
4. Mix well, chill, and serve with tortilla chips.

Makes about 8-10 servings.

DID YOU KNOW...?

- San Diego is the avocado capital of the U.S.

- Varieties of avocados include Bacon, Fuerte, Gwen, Hass, Macarthur, Pinkerton, Reed, and Zulano.

- Corn is available in yellow, white, red, and blue.

- Corn is also known as maize.

- Onions can help cure the common cold.

- Egyptians worshipped onions. They believed the onion symbolized eternal life.

ROASTED VEGGIE SALAD

Ingredients:
- 1 zucchini – cubed
- 6 asparagus stalks – sliced
- 1 cup of baby carrots
- 2 red bell peppers – diced
- 1 sweet potato – cubed
- 3 potatoes – cubed
- ¼ cup of olive oil
- 2 tablespoons of balsamic vinegar
- garlic salt, salt, and black pepper

Preparation:
1. Preheat oven to 475 degrees.
2. In a large bowl, combine all vegetables.
3. In a small bowl, stir together olive oil, vinegar, salt, and pepper.
4. Toss oil mix with vegetables until they are all coated.
5. Spread evenly on a large roasting pan.
6. Sprinkle garlic salt, salt, and black pepper over the vegetables.
7. Roast for 35 to 40 minutes in the oven, stirring every 10 minutes or until vegetables are cooked through and browned.

Makes about 6-8 servings.

DID YOU KNOW...?

- A zucchini has more potassium than a banana.

- The word zucchini comes from "zucca" the Italian word for squash.

- The name, asparagus, comes from the Greek language and means "sprout" or "shoot."

- Asparagus is a member of the Lily family.

- In 1974, a man grew 370 pounds of potatoes on one plant.

- Buds on potatoes are called "eyes."

- The world's largest potato chip measured 23 feet x 14.5 feet.

GO GREEN! RAW SLAW

Ingredients:

- 2 cups of broccoli – chopped
- 1 cup of green beans – chopped
- 1 cup snow peas – chopped
- 1 cup cabbage – chopped
- 1 green pepper – chopped
- 2 cups of fat free sour cream
- ½ cup of white sugar
- ¼ cup of vinegar

Preparation:

1. Chop raw vegetables into small pieces and place in a bowl.
2. Add sour cream, sugar, and vinegar.
3. Mix well and serve cold.

Makes 4-6 servings.

DID YOU KNOW...?

- The average person in the United States eats four and one half pounds of broccoli each year.

- Broccoli got its name from the Latin word bracchium, which means strong arm or branch. They look like little trees!

- California and Arizona produced 100% of the national total.

- Cabbage can be purple or green.

- Cabbage can improve digestion.

- The snow pea is also called the "China mangetout."

LETTUCE EAT! TUNA SALAD SANDWICHES

Ingredients:
- 2 cans chunk light tuna in water
- 1 white onion, diced
- 2 cups of fat free sour cream
- ½ cup of alfalfa sprouts or bean sprouts
- 6-10 leaves of lettuce
- Whole wheat crackers
- Salt and pepper to taste

Preparation:
1. Open tuna cans carefully and drain off water.
2. Place tuna in bowl. Add onion, sour cream, salt and pepper to taste. Mix well.
3. Rinse lettuce leaves and dry thoroughly.
4. Place one piece of lettuce on a plate.
5. Scoop a large serving of the tuna salad onto the lettuce leaf, and top with alfalfa sprouts or bean sprouts.
6. Roll up lettuce leaf to make a tuna wrap. Or, use wheat crackers to make mini tuna sandwiches.

Makes about 6-8 servings.

DID YOU KNOW...?

- Alfalfa is really a member of the pea family.

- Alfalfa sprouts is the top source of anti-oxidant among all vegetables.

- Alfalfa sprouts have nutrients like calcium, folic acid, magnesium, manganese, potassium, silicon, sodium, and zinc.

- Tuna fish can flush toxins out of your liver.

- Tuna fish is high in Vitamins A, B, and E.

- Tuna fish is low in fat and is a fat-burning powerhouse.

BA-GAWK! CHICKEN SALAD SANDWICH/WRAP

Ingredients:

- 2 cups of chicken – cooked and diced
- ¾ cup mayonnaise
- 1 teaspoon of mustard
- 2 eggs – hardboiled and chopped
- ½ cup of celery – diced
- ¼ cup of red onion – diced
- ½ cup of green grapes – chopped
- 4-6 whole wheat tortilla wraps

Preparation:

1. Cook chicken according to package directions (or used canned or pre-cooked chicken). Chop into bite-sized pieces.
2. In a large bowl, mix chicken, mayonnaise, mustard, salt and pepper to taste.
3. Add hardboiled eggs, diced vegetables and chopped grapes.
4. Mix gently and thoroughly.
5. Spoon some chicken salad onto a tortilla wrap and roll it up.

Makes 4-6 servings.

DID YOU KNOW...?

- Chicken is low in fat and high in protein, so it's a good source of energy.

- Chicken contains Vitamins B and E., and other nutrients like riboflavin, niacin, and thiamin.

- A bunch of celery is called a "stalk." Each piece is called a "rib."

- Medieval magicians put celery seeds in their shoes in order to fly.

- Grapes can be green, red, and blue including: Fantasy, Flame, Red Globe, Ribier and Thompson.

BACON LOVER'S SANDWICH

Ingredients:
- 2 slices of whole wheat bread
- 2 slices of lean turkey lunchmeat
- 2 slices of low sodium bacon
- 2 slices of avocado
- 2 slices of tomato
- 2 slices of cheese – provolone or cheddar (or both!)

Preparation:
1. Cook bacon according to package directions and set aside to cool.
2. Slice avocado and tomato.
3. Toast 2 slices of bread.
4. Top toasted bread with cheese slices.
5. Add bacon, tomato, avocado, and turkey.

Makes 1 whole sandwich.

DID YOU KNOW...?

- Bacon is a good source of protein, niacin, phosphorus and selenium.

- September 3rd is international bacon day.

- Turkey breast lunch meat is a good source of protein. Whole wheat bread has roughly 3 times the fiber of white bread.

- Cheese contains calcium and other vitamins and minerals which are good for your bones and teeth.

GIMME 5! BEAN SALAD

Ingredients:
- 1 15 oz. can of garbanzo beans
- 1 15 oz. can pinto beans
- 1 15 oz. can black beans
- 1 15 oz. can kidney beans
- 1 15 oz. can cannellini beans
- 1 cup of white vinegar
- 1 cup of sugar
- 3/4 cup of olive oil

Preparation:
1. Open cans carefully.
2. Rinse beans with cold water and place them in a large bowl.
3. In a separate bowl, mix vinegar, sugar, and oil to make dressing.
4. Pour dressing over the top of the beans.
5. Mix well, chill and serve cold.

Makes 10-12 servings.

DID YOU KNOW...?

- Beans could be called, "healthy people's meat."

- Beans can help reduce heart attacks.

- The pinto bean has more protein than any other bean.

- Pinto beans are also called, "frijoles."

- Black beans are also known as turtle beans, French beans, black kidney beans, black Mexican beans, and Mexican beans

- Cannellini beans are also called, "white kidney beans."

BAKED POTATO SALAD

Ingredients:
- 4 baking potatoes
- 2 cups of fat free sour cream
- 2 cups of shredded cheddar cheese
- 5 slices of bacon – crumbled
- 4 green onions – chopped
- 2 cups of broccoli – chopped

Preparation:
1. Wash vegetables.
2. Poke potatoes with a fork several times.
3. Cook potatoes in microwave for 5 minutes. Use an oven mitt to flip over hot potatoes. Microwave for 5 more minutes.
4. Allow potatoes to cool, carefully cut into bite-sized pieces, and place in a large bowl.
5. Add shredded cheese, sour cream, green onions, broccoli, and bacon crumbles.
6. Mix well. Serve warm or cold.

Makes about 8 servings.

DID YOU KNOW...?

- In 1995, the potato was the first vegetable to be grown in space.

- You can put slices of raw potato on broken bones to speed healing.

- French fries were introduced in the states when Thomas Jefferson was in office between the years of 1801-1809.

- Eating potatoes with other foods can prevent indigestion.

- Potato chips were invented in 1853.

GYRO PASTA SALAD

Ingredients:
- 1 box of spiral pasta
- 1 pound of lean ground beef
- 1 cucumber – diced
- 1 tomato – diced
- ½ white onion – diced
- 2 cups of sour cream
- 1 teaspoon of garlic salt
- Salt and pepper to taste
- 1 head of lettuce, ripped into small pieces
- Pita bread, sliced into strips

Preparation:
1. Cook pasta according to directions.
2. Drain noodles and place in a large bowl.
3. Add sour cream, garlic salt, and pepper. Mix well.
4. Cook lean ground beef and drain off grease. Add to noodles.
5. Add cucumber, tomato, and onion.
6. Mix well.
7. Serve on a bed of lettuce with a side of pita bread strips.

Makes about 8 servings.

DID YOU KNOW...?

- Beef contains protein that can help build muscle.

- Beef has zinc, Vitamin B12, and iron.

- Lean beef has more Vitamin B12, more zinc, and more iron than the same size serving of skinless chicken breast.

- The flavor of a cucumber comes from its seeds.

- The inside of a cucumber can be up to 20 degrees cooler than the outside air.

RICARDO'S MEXICAN PASTA SALAD

Ingredients:
- 1 box of wheel pasta
- 2 cups of shredded cheddar cheese
- 2 cups of fat free sour cream
- 1 taco seasoning packet
- 1 tomato – diced
- 1 green pepper – diced
- 5 green onions – diced
- 3 cups of cooked chicken – diced
- ½ can of black olives
- 1 can of black beans – rinsed
- Taco chips

Preparation:
1. Cook pasta according to directions, drain with water, and place in a large bowl.
2. Add cheese, sour cream, and taco seasoning packet. Mix well.
3. Add tomato, green pepper, onion, chicken, olives, and beans. Mix well again, stirring gently.
4. Serve on a bed of taco chips.

Makes about 8 servings.

DID YOU KNOW...?

- Chinese people were making noodles as early as 3000 BC.

- Noodles are low in fat and low in sodium.

- The average American eats 20 pounds of pasta each year.

- Tomatoes can lower your risk of cancer.

- In the U.S., tomatoes are eaten more than any other fruit or vegetable.

- Florida is the number one producer of fresh market tomatoes.

LEAN BURGER PASTA SALAD

Ingredients:
- 1 box of macaroni pasta
- 1 ½ cups of mayonnaise
- 2 cups of shredded cheddar cheese
- 1 pound of lean ground beef
- 1 cup of dill pickle chips
- 1 tomato – diced
- 1 onion – diced
- 1 head of lettuce – shredded
- Ketchup
- Mustard
- Potato sticks or potato chips

Preparation:
1. Cook pasta according to directions, drain, and place in a large bowl.
2. Add mayo and cheese. Mix well.
3. Cook lean ground beef, drain off grease, and add to noodles.
4. Add tomato, onion, and dill pickle chips. Mix well.
5. Serve on a bed of lettuce, and top with potato sticks.
6. Add a decorative squirt of ketchup and mustard on top.

Makes 6-8 servings.

DID YOU KNOW...?

- In America, dill pickles are twice as popular as sweet pickles.

- The largest hamburger on record weighed 5,000 pounds.

- The average American eats 3 hamburgers per week.

- The first fast-food burger made in 1921 cost 5 cents.

- The Hamburger Hall of Fame is located in Wisconsin.

MYSTERY OF THE MISSING TOMATO PESTO

Ingredients:

- 1 box of angel hair pasta
- 2 large tomatoes – chopped
- 1 cup of olive oil
- 1 tablespoon of garlic salt
- ½ cup of parmesan cheese
- 3 cups of green beans – raw or cooked

Preparation:

1. Cook pasta according to directions, drain, and set aside.
2. In a blender, mix tomatoes, olive oil, garlic salt, and parmesan cheese until well blended.
3. Pour tomato pesto over angel hair pasta.
4. Serve warm or cold with a side of fresh green beans.

Makes 4-6 servings.

DID YOU KNOW...?

- The Aztecs made what may be the first salsa – tomatoes prepared with peppers, corn, and salt.

- China is the world's largest producer of tomatoes.

- The leaves of a tomato plant are poisonous.

- Green beans can actually be green, yellow, purple, or speckled in those colors.

- Green beans vary in size, but the average length is about 4 inches.

GINO'S HOMEMADE PIZZA

Ingredients:

- 1 package of yeast
- 2 ½ cups of flour
- ½ teaspoon of garlic salt
- 2 tablespoons of oil
- 2-3 cups of shredded mozzarella cheese
- 2 cups of tomato sauce
- ½ cup of mushrooms – sliced
- ½ cup of green peppers – diced
- ½ cup of pineapples – diced
- Pepperoni slices

Preparation:

1. Dissolve yeast in 1 cup of warm water (not too hot, not too cold).
2. Add flour, garlic salt, and oil. Knead until dough forms.
3. Cover and let dough rise for 10 minutes.
4. Roll out dough with rolling pin. Place in pie pan. Poke holes in dough with a fork. Pre-cook dough in 375 degree oven for about 7 minutes.
5. Carefully remove dough from oven. Add sauce, cheese, and toppings of your choice. Return to oven and cook for 12 minutes.
6. Remove cooked pizza from oven and allow it to cool before serving.

Makes two large pizzas.

DID YOU KNOW...?

- Throughout history, mushrooms were thought to have medicinal powers.

- Peppers are a good source of Vitamin C.

- There are four types of pineapples including Gold, smooth Cayenne, Red Spanish and Sugar Loaf.

- A pineapple can weigh up to 10 pounds.

- A pineapple takes about 18 months to grow.

NANA'S LEFT-OVER TURKEY AND VEGETABLE SOUP

Ingredients:

- 2 cups of roasted turkey – chopped into bite sized chunks
- 2 cups of turkey broth
- 2 cups of carrots – diced
- 1 yellow onion – diced
- 4 celery stalks – diced
- 1 can of corn – rinsed
- 2 cups of cabbage – diced
- 1 cup of lima beans
- 1 tablespoon of garlic salt
- Pepper
- Salt

Preparation:

1. Dice vegetables and place them together in a large bowl.
2. In a large cooking pot, pour 2 cups of turkey broth, 4 cups of water, and garlic salt. Bring to a boil.
3. Carefully add vegetables and turkey chunks.
4. Turn down to low heat and let the soup simmer for 20 minutes.
5. Add salt and pepper to taste.
6. Serve with whole wheat crackers or oyster crackers.

Makes 8-10 servings.

DID YOU KNOW...?

- Lima beans are rich source of antioxidants, vitamins, minerals, and fiber.

- Carrots help improve eyesight, especially at night.

- Carrots help keep your skin and hair healthy.

- Carrots have the highest beta-carotene of any vegetable.

- Holtville, California dubs itself "The Carrot Capital of the World."

- The largest cabbage on record weighed 123 pounds.

- A cabbage can grow in three months time.

CRUMB'S CORNFLAKE CHICKEN AND SWEET POTATO BAKES

Ingredients:
- 1 ½ cups of cornflakes – crushed
- 8-10 chicken tenderloins
- 1 egg
- ½ cup of milk
- ¾ cup of parmesan cheese
- 2 large sweet potatoes
- 1 cup butter
- Brown sugar
- Cinnamon

Preparation:
1. In a small bowl, mix egg and milk until well blended. In another bowl, crush cornflakes and mix with parmesan cheese.
2. Grease a small baking dish. Use a fork to dip the chicken in the egg mix, then the cornflake mix, and place in the baking dish.
3. Place chicken in oven at 350 degrees and cook for 20 minutes.
4. Chop sweet potatoes into bite-sized wedges. Mix with butter, sugar, and cinnamon. Microwave for 5 minutes.
5. Remove from microwave and pour into a greased baking dish. Cook in a 350 degree oven for 10 minutes.

Makes 8-10 servings.

DID YOU KNOW...?

- Milk contains proteins, calcium, phosphorus, magnesium, and potassium.

- Milk promotes healthy skin and eyes.

- The sweet potato is a part of the morning glory family.

- Sweet potatoes are also called "yams."

- There are three types of sweet potatoes grown: rose or red-skinned, orange-fleshed, and white or tan-fleshed.

CHEESY MAC AND VEGGIES

Ingredients:

- 1 (16 oz.) package of macaroni
- 2 cups of shredded cheddar cheese
- 1 cup of Havarti cheese
- 2 tablespoons of parmesan cheese
- 2 ½ cup of milk
- 3 tablespoons of margarine
- 2 cups of chicken broth
- 1 small tomato – diced
- 1 cup of broccoli – diced
- 2 cups of green beans

Preparation:

1. Cook the macaroni according to the package directions, rinse, and place in a lightly-greased, oven-safe bowl. Mix in broccoli and tomato.
2. In a saucepan over low heat, melt the margarine. Add the chicken broth and milk.
3. Stir in the cheese, saving a little to sprinkle on top. Stir until cheese is melted then pour over macaroni.
4. Bake for 30 minutes at 350 degrees.
5. Serve with a side of green beans.

Makes 4-6 servings.

DID YOU KNOW...?

- There is a crayon color called "macaroni and cheese."

- There are two restaurants in New York that serve only macaroni and cheese.

- Macaroni and cheese is the number one cheese recipe in the United States.

- Macaroni and cheese is one of the top ten comfort foods in the United States.

- Kraft sells more than one million boxes of macaroni and cheese every day.

GHETTI AND TURKEY MEATBALLS

Ingredients:
- 1 pound of ground turkey
- 1 egg
- ½ cup of potato chips – crushed
- Garlic salt, salt, and black pepper to taste
- 1 16.oz package of spaghetti
- I jar of pasta sauce
- 1 large tomato – diced
- ½ white onion – diced

Preparation:
1. In a glass bowl, mix the ground turkey egg, bread crumbs and a sprinkle of garlic salt, pepper, and salt.
2. With your hands, shape the meat into balls. Cook in a skillet at medium heat until fully cooked (about 5-8 minutes). Drain fat.
3. Cook spaghetti according to package directions. Drain.
4. Warm pasta sauce, Add onions and tomatoes.
5. Place spaghetti on plate, top with sauce and meatballs.

Makes about 6 servings.

DID YOU KNOW...?

- There are 42 calories in one turkey meatball.

- Meatballs can be made with beef, chicken, turkey, or pork.

- Many nations and cultures make meatballs with their own kinds of sauces and gravies.

- Originally, meatballs were served alone and spaghetti was served alone. It wasn't until much later that the two were served together.

- In Afghanistan, meatballs are not grilled and placed on top of pizza.

- In October 2009 an Italian eatery in Concord, New Hampshire set the record for the biggest meatball at 222.5 pounds.

CHINESE RICE WITH TOFU VEGETABLE STIR FRY

Ingredients:
- 1 package whole grain rice
- 1 cup tofu – firm, chopped
- 1 cup cabbage – shredded or chopped
- 1 cup bok choy – chopped
- 1 cup green onion – diced
- 1 cup carrots – diced
- 1 cup green peppers – diced
- 1 cup broccoli – chopped
- ¼ cup of soy sauce
- ½ cup of olive oil

Preparation:
1. Cook rice according to package directions. Set aside.
2. In a large skillet or wok, warm olive oil to medium heat.
3. Add tofu and cook until lightly browned.
4. Add vegetables, garlic salt, and soy sauce then stir.
5. Cover and steam in pan for 3 minutes.
6. Serve vegetables over rice. Season with soy sauce.

Makes about 8 servings.

DID YOU KNOW...?

- Bok choy is also known as Chinese cabbage.

- Bok choy is very nutritious, it's high in Vitamin A, Vitamin C, potassium and calcium.

- Tofu acts like a sponge and has the miraculous ability to soak up any flavor that is added to it.

- Tofu is also known as soybean curd.

- Green onions are also known as scallions.

- On a green onion, the white bulb and the green stalk are both edible.

NANA'S APPLE PECAN PIE

Ingredients:
- 2 tablespoons of flour
- 1 cup of sugar
- ¼ cup of pecans – chopped
- ½ teaspoon of cinnamon
- 6 Red Delicious apples – peeled and sliced
- 1 ½ tablespoons of butter
- 2 ready-made pie crusts

Preparation:
1. In a large bowl, combine flour, sugar, pecans, and cinnamon.
2. Add apple slices and mix well.
3. Place one pie crust dough piece in a 9 inch pie pan.
4. Pour in apple mixture.
5. Cover with second pie dough.
6. Melt butter and brush on top of the pie crust.
7. Bake at 350 degrees for 45 minutes.

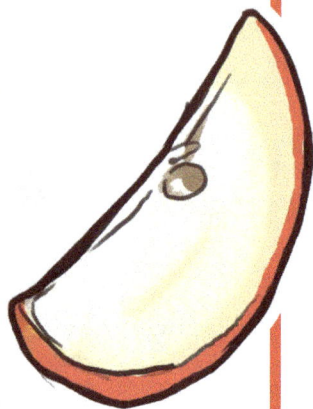

Makes about 8 servings.

DID YOU KNOW...?

- The science of apple growing is called pomology.

- An American eats about 19 pounds of apples every year.

- It takes the energy from 50 leaves to produce one apple.

- The largest apple ever picked weighed three pounds, two ounces.

- The skin of an apple contains more antioxidants and fiber than the flesh.

- The apple is the official state fruit of Washington, New York, Rhode Island, and West Virginia.

- China produces more apples than any other country.

HEALTHY BENJI'S MIX MANIA

Ingredients:

- ½ cup of raisins
- ½ cup of chocolate chips
- 1 cup of cereal pieces – like Cheerios, Rice Chex, or Kix
- ½ cup of dried cranberries
- ½ cup of dried blueberries
- ½ cup of dried fruit pieces – like apricots, bananas, or mangos
- ½ cup of peanuts or almond
- 1 cup of pretzel sticks
- ½ cup of mini marshmallows
- ½ cup of goldfish crackers

Preparation:

1. Open a ½ gallon zip-close bag.
2. Add raisins, chocolate chips, cranberries, blueberries, dried fruit, and nuts.
3. Close bag and shake to mix.
4. Open bag and add the cereal pieces, pretzels, marshmallows, and crackers.
5. Close bag and shake to mix again.

Makes about 10 servings.

DID YOU KNOW...?

- Cranberries are a good source of Vitamin C.

- Another name for cranberries is "bounceberries" because they bounce when they are ripe.

- Cranberries are grown on sandy bogs or marshes. Because cranberries float, some bogs are flooded when the fruit is ready for harvesting.

- Michigan is the nation's top producer of blueberries. Apricots are a good source of Vitamins A and C, as well as potassium and fiber.

TUTTI FRUITY ICE CREAM PIE

Ingredients:
- 3 cups vanilla frozen yogurt
- ½ cup of fresh or frozen cherries – pitted
- ½ cup of fresh peaches – diced
- ½ cup of pineapple – diced
- 1 chocolate-cookie pie crust

Preparation:
1. In a large bowl, combine ice cream, cherries, peaches, and pineapples. Stir gently to mix.
2. Pour mix into the graham cracker crust.
3. Freeze until the pie is firm, at least 4 hours.

Makes about 8 servings.

DID YOU KNOW...?

- There are two kinds of cherries – tart and sweet.
- Tart cherries can help relieve a headache.
- Michigan produces the most cherries of any state.
- The pineapple was first called, "anana" which is the Caribbean word for "excellent fruit."
- The pineapple is actually a cluster of 100-200 fruitlets.
- The world's largest peach weighed 10,000 pounds.
- Georgia is known as the Peach State.

HEALTHY BENJI'S POWER DRINK BY DR. OZ.

Make the breakfast drink that Dr. Oz swears by! This "green drink" is high in fiber, low-calorie and rich in vitamins.

Ingredients
- 2 cups spinach
- 1/2 cucumber
- 1/4 head of celery
- 1/2 bunch parsley
- 1 bunch mint
- 3 carrots
- 2 apples
- 1/4 orange
- 1/4 lime
- 1/4 lemon
- 1/4 pineapple

Preparation:
4.   Combine all ingredients in a blender.

Makes approximately 28-30 ounces, or 3-4 servings.

GLOSSARY

Aroma – 'a·ro·ma', smell, sepecially a pleasant one 5

Bratwurst – German sausage also known as a brat,
usually composed of veal, pork or beef 12, 36, 58

Buklawa -ˈbɑːkləvɑ', a Mediterranean rich, sweet pastry
made of layers of phyllo pastry filled with chopped nuts
and sweetened with syrup or honey. 14

Chow Mein – 'chāu-mèing' – a Chineese dish of stir-fried
noodles with meat 7, 29, 52

Ditalini – "little thimbles" in Italian, is most typically used
in the Campania region of Italy, where it graces Pasta e
Fagioli, minestrone and other classic soups – even a
simple bowl of plain broth. 10, 33, 56

Edamame Bean – a preparation of immature soybeans
in the pod, found in the cuisine of Japan, China and
Hawaii 7

Empanada – Spanish stuffed bread or pastry baked
or fried 17

Ethnic – 'eth·nic' – distinctive cultural
traits. 2, 3, 22, 24, 25, 47, 50, 69

Jambalaya – Louisiana Creole dish made with
shrimp, onions, tomatoes, celery, and spices . . . 19, 43, 66

Kabobs – vegetables and meat on wooden sticks . . 13, 37, 60

Khao Phat Kai – Thai fried rice, a variety of fried rice
typical of central Thai cuisine 8, 30, 53

Kielbasa – a garlic-flavored Polish pork sausage that
can be boiled, boiled and browned or smoked . . . 11, 35, 58

Lasagna – a dish made with pasta in several layers
interspersed with layers of various ingredients and
sauces. 9, 33, 55

Linguini – a form of Italian pasta, flat like fettuccine
and trenette, wider than spaghetti, about 4mm,
but not as wide as fettuccine. 9, 33, 55

Mardi Gras – events of the Carnival celebrations, beginning
on or after Epiphany and culminating on the day before Ash
Wednesday. Mardi gras is French for Fat Tuesday, referring
to the practice of the last night of eating richer, fatty foods
before the ritual fasting of the Lenten season, which begins
on Ash Wednesday 19, 43, 66

Miso Soup – a traditional Japanese soup consisting of
a stock called "dashi" into which softened miso paste is
mixed. 7, 29, 52

Nifty – 'nif•ty' – something clever, neat, or excellent,
especially a witticism 6, 21, 45

Paczek – A round Polish pastry similar to a doughnut, usually filled with fruit and topped with sugar or icing.. . . . 11, 35, 58

Pad Thai – Phat Thai, "fried Thai style"; Vietnamese dish of stir-fried pho noodles, a type of rice noodle, with eggs, fish sauce, tamarind juice, red chili pepper, plus any combination of bean sprouts, shrimp, chicken, hot dogs or tofu, garnished with crushed peanuts, coriander and lime. 8, 30, 53

Pecan Pie – is a pie made primarily with corn syrup and pecan nuts. 19, 43, 66

Penne – a type of Italian pasta with cylinder-shaped pieces. 9, 33, 55

Pepperoni – pepperoni sausage, is an Italian-American variety of salami, usually made from cured pork and beef.. . . . . 9, 32, 55

Pierogi – dumplings of unleavened dough, first boiled, then they are baked or fried usually in butter with onions, traditionally stuffed with potato filling, sauerkraut, ground meat, cheese, or fruit. 11

Pita Bread – a round pocket bread widely consumed in many Middle Eastern, Mediterranean, and Balkan cuisines, created by steam, which puffs up the dough. As the bread cools and flattens, a pocket is left in the middle. 13, 37, 60, 61

Pizza – 'pittsa' is an oven-baked, flat, round bread typically topped with a tomato sauce, cheese and various toppings. 9, 20, 32, 44, 55, 67

www.ingramcontent.com/pod-product-compliance
Lightning Source LLC
Chambersburg PA
CBHW050640150426

42813CB00054B/1126